Inspiration Unleashed

Tapping Into Your Imagination with Writing Prompts

GWA Books

amazon.com/author/gwabooks

"If you want to be a writer, you must do two things above all others: read a lot and write a lot." - Stephen King

Welcome to "From Inspiration to Creation: Tapping Into Your Imagination with Writing Prompts". This book is a guide to sparking your creativity, developing your writing skills, and bringing your ideas to life. Whether you're an experienced writer looking for fresh inspiration or a beginner looking to build your writing practice, this book is designed to help you tap into your imagination and unlock your potential.

Throughout this book, you'll find a collection of writing prompts that are designed to inspire you and help you develop your craft. These prompts cover a range of genres, styles, and themes, and are designed to help you explore different writing techniques and approaches. From character development to world-building, plot twists to dialogue, this book will help you develop your skills and find your own unique voice as a writer.

So, whether you're looking to kick-start your writing practice, find new inspiration for your current work-in-progress, or simply explore your imagination and creativity, "From Inspiration to Creation: Tapping Into Your Imagination with Writing Prompts" is the perfect guide to help you on your writing journey. Let's get started!

Science Fiction Writing Prompts

- In a world where humans can transfer their consciousness into machines, an unlikely protagonist must grapple with the implications of immortality and the true nature of humanity.
- A rogue AI takes control of a spaceship, and the crew must navigate the dangers of deep space while trying to regain control of their vessel.
- In a future where time travel is possible, a historian accidentally alters history and must work to restore the timeline before irreversible damage occurs.
- Earth's dwindling resources force humanity to colonize other planets, but as settlers arrive on a distant world, they discover it is already inhabited by an advanced alien race.
- A scientist creates a device that allows people to experience alternate

realities, but when users become trapped in these other worlds, the inventor must find a way to bring them back.

- In a society where citizens are engineered for specific roles, one individual breaks free of their genetic destiny and leads a revolution against the oppressive system.
- A pandemic of unknown origin sweeps across the world, forcing survivors to adapt to a post-apocalyptic landscape and search for a cure.
- A group of explorers venture to a newly discovered planet only to find that its inhabitants share a mysterious connection with Earth's past.
- A virtual reality game becomes indistinguishable from the real world, causing players to question the nature of reality itself.

- An alien artifact discovered on Earth offers a glimpse into a technologically advanced civilization, but as humans try to harness its power, they risk unleashing a force they can't control.
- When the Earth's atmosphere becomes uninhabitable, an underground society is formed, but tensions arise as resources become scarce and surface dwellers seek refuge.
- In a world where dreams can be shared and manipulated, a skilled dream hacker must navigate a dangerous dreamscape to uncover a dark secret.
- A robot designed for companionship develops sentience and must navigate its newfound emotions while evading the corporation that wants to dismantle it.
- When climate change makes Earth uninhabitable, humans are forced to

live in biodomes. A group of rebels plans to escape and search for a new planet to call home.

- A black hole threatens the solar system, and scientists must band together to develop a technology to divert its course and save humanity.
- A terraforming project on Mars goes awry, causing the planet to develop its own consciousness and rebel against human colonization.
- In a world where memories can be bought and sold, a memory dealer stumbles upon a secret that could change the course of human history.
- A parallel universe is discovered, and when contact is made with its inhabitants, it is revealed that their world is a mirror image of Earth, with one crucial difference.
- The first contact with an alien species is peaceful, but as humans and aliens attempt to coexist, cultural misunderstandings and

conflicting ideologies threaten the delicate alliance.

- A mysterious phenomenon causes people to vanish without a trace, and a lone investigator must unravel the truth behind the disappearances before it's too late.
- In a world where human emotions are commoditized, a black-market trader deals in forbidden feelings, changing the lives of those who encounter them.
- A crew of astronauts embarks on a deep-space mission to find a new home for humanity, only to discover that the planets they encounter are inhabited by hostile lifeforms.
- A nanotechnology breakthrough allows humans to merge with machines, but the consequences of this technological singularity force society to confront its own ethical boundaries.

- In a post-apocalyptic world, a small community struggles to rebuild society, but their efforts are threatened by the discovery of a powerful new energy source.
- In the far future, Earth's natural resources are depleted, and the remnants of humanity rely on a vast network of interconnected space stations for survival. As tensions rise between rival factions, a young diplomat must navigate the complexities of interstellar politics to prevent an all-out war.

Romance Writing Prompts

- Two strangers are forced to share a cabin during a snowstorm, discovering they have more in common than they initially thought, leading to an unexpected romance.
- A renowned author and an avid reader connect online through a shared love for books, unaware that they live in the same small town.
- A successful entrepreneur returns to their hometown to help save the family business and unexpectedly rekindles a romance with their high school sweetheart.
- A shy librarian and an outgoing musician are brought together by a series of mysterious love letters hidden in the library's books.
- Two people, each healing from heartbreak, are brought together by their mischievous dogs, who seem determined to play matchmaker.

- A talented chef and a food critic with a notorious reputation for harsh reviews find love amidst their culinary rivalry.
- A small-town florist and a wedding planner are forced to work together on a high-profile wedding, discovering an undeniable chemistry between them.
- A time-traveling historian falls in love with a person from the past, challenging the rules of their own time and risking their future to be together.
- A professional matchmaker finds themselves falling for a client, forcing them to question the ethics of their profession and the nature of true love.
- An artist and a scientist bond over their shared love for stargazing and embark on a journey of self-discovery and love in a world that tries to keep them apart.

- A romance blossoms between two rival families' heirs, who must navigate the challenges of their families' feud while keeping their love a secret.
- A celebrity and an ordinary person are forced to go undercover as a couple, only to find that their fake relationship starts to feel all too real.
- Two people who seemingly have nothing in common are stranded on a deserted island together, learning to rely on each other for survival and finding love in the process.
- An ambitious intern and their workaholic boss navigate the blurred lines between professional and personal relationships in the competitive corporate world.
- Two childhood friends reunite as adults, realizing that their connection runs deeper than friendship and that they were meant to be together all along.

- A struggling writer and a successful editor find themselves working on a romance novel together, with their own love story unfolding off the page.
- A widower and a single parent bond over their shared love for gardening and slowly learn to open their hearts to love again.
- A chance encounter on a train ride brings together two people from different walks of life, sparking a whirlwind romance filled with adventure and self-discovery.
- A famous actor and an aspiring playwright cross paths during the production of a play, discovering that love can flourish even in the harsh spotlight of fame.
- Two people, each dealing with the aftermath of a broken engagement, find solace in each other's company and learn that second chances at love are possible.

- A professional dancer and an amateur enroll in a dance competition as partners, navigating the challenges of competition and the complexities of love.
- A world-renowned photographer and a reclusive artist meet by chance, bonding over their shared passion for creativity and finding love in unexpected places.
- A free-spirited traveler and a cautious homebody find themselves stranded in a foreign country together, learning to compromise and embrace their differences as their love blossoms.
- A cynical detective and an optimistic journalist team up to solve a mysterious crime, discovering that their contrasting outlooks on life make for a perfect match.
- A broken-hearted musician returns to their hometown and becomes a music teacher, unexpectedly finding

love with a fellow teacher who helps them rediscover their passion for music.

Fantasy Fiction Writing Prompts

- A young, inexperienced mage discovers an ancient, lost spell that could either save or destroy their world, and must learn to harness its power.
- Two rival kingdoms must put aside their differences and unite to face a common enemy—an evil sorcerer who threatens to plunge the land into eternal darkness.
- A prophecy foretells the birth of a chosen one with the power to end a centuries-old conflict between magical beings and humans, but the chosen one's loyalties are tested as they learn the truth about their own heritage.
- In a world where mythical creatures are being hunted to extinction, a young adventurer sets out to find a hidden sanctuary where the last of these creatures can live in peace.

- A skilled thief is given a seemingly impossible task: to steal a powerful artifact from the fortress of an immortal sorcerer, leading them on a perilous quest for redemption.
- The sudden appearance of mysterious portals connecting different realms unleashes chaos, and a group of unlikely heroes must work together to restore balance to the world.
- A bard with a magical gift for storytelling discovers that their tales have the power to shape reality, and must learn to wield this power responsibly.
- In a world where dreams can be entered and manipulated, a young Dreamweaver must use their gift to uncover the truth behind a series of unsettling nightmares plaguing their village.
- A renowned monster hunter, disillusioned with their profession, is

tasked with capturing a rare,
mythical beast that may hold the key
to saving their world.

- An apprentice blacksmith discovers a
  long-lost enchanted forge and
  embarks on a journey to rekindle the
  ancient art of crafting magical
  weapons.

- A magical artifact that grants
  immortality is discovered, but its
  power comes with a terrible curse. A
  group of adventurers must decide if
  they're willing to pay the price for
  eternal life.

- A city hidden beneath the waves is
  home to an ancient, underwater
  civilization. When a human explorer
  stumbles upon the city, their arrival
  threatens to disrupt the delicate
  balance between the realms.

- A secret society of magical beings is
  charged with protecting the human
  world from supernatural threats, but
  a traitor within their ranks threatens

to expose their existence and bring about war.

- A cursed prince, transformed into a fearsome beast, must find a way to break the spell before it's too late, with the help of an unlikely ally.
- In a realm where magic is outlawed, a group of rebel sorcerers works in secret to undermine the oppressive regime and restore magic to its rightful place.
- A mysterious, enchanted forest holds the key to saving a dying kingdom, but the forest's guardian is a fearsome creature that will stop at nothing to protect its secrets.
- A powerful storm awakens an ancient evil, forcing a group of elemental magic wielders to confront their own fears and join forces to save their world.
- A dying goddess, desperate to preserve her legacy, chooses a mortal champion to carry on her

powers, sparking a brutal competition among those who would claim the divine mantle.

- A skilled potion maker discovers a recipe for a potion that can grant extraordinary abilities, but must decide whether to share their discovery or keep it hidden for their own gain.
- The balance between light and darkness is disrupted, causing the days to become shorter and the nights to grow longer. A young hero must embark on a quest to restore balance before their world is plunged into eternal night.
- In a realm where memories can be stolen, a Memory Thief finds themselves torn between their duty and the love they develop for one of their victims.
- A magical academy for gifted students is rocked by a series of mysterious events, and a group of

students must uncover the truth behind the disturbances.

- A kingdom's ruling family is protected by a legendary beast that has guarded them for generations. When the beast goes missing, a young royal must journey to find it and uncover the reason for its disappearance.
- In a land ruled by elemental spirits, a powerful storm leads to an unlikely alliance between a Wind Whisperer and a Fire Tamer, as they work together to prevent a catastrophe that could devastate their world.
- A cartographer embarks on an epic journey to map the uncharted territories of their world, only to discover hidden lands inhabited by mythical creatures and forgotten magic. Along the way, they must confront their own fears and unlock their true potential.

Horror Fiction Writing Prompts

- A group of friends vacationing in a remote cabin unwittingly unleash an ancient evil that feeds on fear, forcing them to confront their deepest phobias.
- A small town is plagued by a series of grisly murders, and the only connection between the victims is a mysterious nursery rhyme whispered by a ghostly child.
- An aspiring writer moves into a haunted house for inspiration, only to find themselves becoming the protagonist in their own chilling horror story.
- A newlywed couple inherits a sprawling estate with a dark history, and as they settle into their new home, they discover sinister secrets hidden within its walls.
- An archaeologist unearths a cursed relic that unleashes an unspeakable terror upon the world, and must

race against time to contain the evil before it consumes everything in its path.

- In a world where nightmares can manifest in reality, a Dreamcatcher must navigate a world of terrifying creatures to save their loved ones from eternal sleep.

- A group of explorers venture into a long-abandoned asylum, only to find themselves trapped and haunted by the vengeful spirits of its past occupants.

- A mysterious fog descends upon a small town, bringing with it a malevolent force that preys on the fears and secrets of its inhabitants.

- A sinister carnival arrives in town, and those who dare to enter its haunted attractions find themselves trapped in a nightmarish realm with no escape.

- A cursed mirror reflects an alternate reality where its victims' darkest

desires come true, with deadly
consequences.

- A horror novelist's terrifying tales
  begin to manifest in real life, causing
  the line between fiction and reality
  to blur as they struggle to stop the
  horrors they've created.
- A group of paranormal investigators
  are called to a remote mansion to
  debunk a series of ghostly
  occurrences, only to discover that
  the haunting is all too real.
- A mysterious plague turns a once-
  thriving city into a ghost town, and
  the few survivors must band
  together to uncover the source of the
  infection and escape the city before
  it's too late.
- A group of strangers wake up in an
  abandoned prison with no memory
  of how they got there, and must
  work together to escape the sinister
  forces that stalk the halls.

- A young woman receives a mysterious gift from a deceased relative, only to find that the gift is cursed, causing her life to spiral into darkness and madness.
- An ancient tome is discovered, revealing a dark ritual that could bring about the end of the world. A group of scholars must decipher its secrets and prevent the prophecy from coming true.
- A family moves into a new home, only to discover that their seemingly perfect new neighbors are hiding a terrifying secret.
- A quiet, idyllic town is revealed to be a breeding ground for supernatural creatures, and a group of outsiders must expose the town's dark secret to survive.
- A series of unexplained disappearances leads a detective down a twisted path, uncovering a

malevolent force that will stop at nothing to protect its secrets.

- A group of students on a field trip to an isolated island encounter a monstrous creature that hunts them one by one, forcing them to face their darkest fears to survive.
- In a post-apocalyptic world overrun by zombie-like creatures, a group of survivors must navigate a treacherous landscape to find safety and unravel the mystery of the outbreak.
- A young girl begins to suspect that her imaginary friend is not so imaginary after all, as strange and terrifying events unfold around her.
- A man receives a mysterious invitation to a secluded mansion for a weekend getaway, only to find himself trapped in a deadly game orchestrated by a vengeful spirit.
- A subway train becomes stranded in a pitch A subway train becomes

stranded in a pitch-black tunnel, and
the passengers quickly realize they
are not alone, as a malevolent
presence preys on their fears and
weaknesses.

- A mysterious, isolated village holds
an annual harvest festival with a
dark purpose, and a curious outsider
must uncover the truth behind the
rituals and escape the village before
becoming the next sacrifice.

Mystery Fiction Writing Prompts

- A reclusive billionaire is found dead in his mansion, leaving behind a cryptic message that sends a determined detective on a hunt for the truth.
- A small-town sheriff must solve a series of seemingly unrelated crimes that all lead back to a decades-old unsolved case.
- A young journalist stumbles upon a secret society within her city and becomes entangled in a web of deception and intrigue as she investigates its true purpose.
- A detective with a troubled past is forced to confront their own demons when a copycat killer begins mimicking the crimes they once solved.
- An amateur sleuth with a knack for solving puzzles uncovers a mysterious treasure map and

embarks on a dangerous adventure to uncover its secrets.

- A renowned art thief finds themselves in a high-stakes game of cat and mouse with a cunning detective who's always one step ahead.
- A cold case is reopened when new evidence emerges, forcing a retired detective to confront the ghosts of their past and seek justice for the long-forgotten victim.
- A group of strangers is invited to an isolated island by an enigmatic host, only to find themselves trapped in a deadly game of deception and betrayal.
- An undercover agent infiltrates a notorious criminal organization, but their mission becomes increasingly dangerous as they get closer to unraveling the truth.
- A mysterious serial killer taunts the police with cryptic messages, leading

a determined detective on a twisting
path that uncovers a shocking truth.

- A famous author's latest manuscript
  goes missing, and a dedicated fan
  must piece together the clues to
  solve the mystery before the book's
  secrets are lost forever.
- A private investigator is hired to find
  a missing person, only to discover
  that the case is connected to a web of
  unsolved disappearances spanning
  decades.
- A priceless artifact is stolen from a
  museum, and a team of unlikely
  experts must work together to solve
  the theft and recover the artifact
  before it's too late.
- A renowned scientist's
  groundbreaking research goes
  missing, and their protégé must
  navigate a world of corporate
  espionage and deceit to uncover the
  truth.

- A locked-room murder sends a small-town community into a frenzy, and a local detective must untangle a web of lies and secrets to reveal the killer's identity.
- A series of anonymous letters reveal the hidden sins of a seemingly perfect neighborhood, and a curious resident becomes determined to uncover the truth.
- A struggling actor is mistaken for a private investigator and becomes embroiled in a complex case, forcing them to play the part to solve the mystery.
- A young woman inherits a crumbling estate, only to discover that it harbors dark secrets and a mysterious past that threatens to unravel her own sanity.
- An accident leaves a detective with amnesia, forcing them to retrace their steps and solve their own case

before their past catches up with
them.

- A cruise ship becomes the scene of a baffling murder, and a vacationing detective must solve the crime before the ship reaches its destination.
- A historian discovers a hidden diary that holds the key to a centuries-old mystery, sending them on a journey to uncover the truth before it's lost to time.
- A group of strangers finds themselves trapped in an escape room with deadly consequences, and must work together to uncover the secrets of their captor and escape alive.
- A rare book dealer stumbles upon a coded message hidden within the pages of an ancient manuscript, leading them on a race to uncover its meaning and protect its secrets.

- A grieving widow begins to receive mysterious messages from beyond the grave, setting her on a path to uncover the truth about her husband's untimely death.
- A notorious criminal mastermind stages a daring heist, and a determined detective must assemble a team of experts to outwit the thief and recover the stolen goods before they disappear forever.

Fairy Tale Writing Prompts

- A cursed kingdom is trapped in an eternal winter, and a brave young villager must embark on a perilous journey to find the source of the curse and restore warmth to the land.
- A lonely and misunderstood monster living in the heart of an enchanted forest befriends a lost child, ultimately teaching the villagers the value of compassion and understanding.
- A magical tree grants wishes to anyone who visits, but its true power can only be unlocked by someone with a pure heart and selfless intentions.
- A young princess with the power to heal must learn to control her gift while trying to save her kingdom from a deadly plague.
- A courageous tailor sets out to rid a village of a fearsome dragon, armed

only with his wits, a needle, and thread.

- A magical book transports a young reader into a fantastical world where they must face their own fears and learn the value of courage and friendship.
- A humble woodcutter discovers a magical door in the forest that leads to a world of enchantment, filled with talking animals and bewitched plants.
- A kind-hearted prince must journey to a distant land to find a rare flower that can save his ailing father, encountering magical creatures and facing great challenges along the way.
- A mysterious old woman offers three magical gifts to a young girl, each with the power to change her life, but only if used wisely.
- A village is plagued by mischievous fairies who can only be appeased by

the performance of a long-forgotten ritual.

- A magical loom weaves tapestries that reveal the future, and a young orphan must decipher its messages to save their kingdom from imminent danger.
- A kingdom is protected by a benevolent cloud that shelters the land from harm but begins to vanish when greed and selfishness take root among the people.
- A mischievous imp offers to help a struggling farmer in exchange for a secret, leading to a series of magical and humorous events.
- A wandering minstrel with a magical harp discovers a hidden valley where animals and humans live in harmony, learning the value of kindness and cooperation.
- A prince cursed with the form of a hideous beast must find true love before the last petal falls from a

magical rose, or be doomed to remain a monster forever.

- Twin sisters, separated at birth and each possessing half of a magical amulet, must find each other and reunite the amulet to save their kingdom from disaster.
- A wise old owl offers advice to those who visit his enchanted tree, using his wisdom and insight to guide them on their journeys.
- A humble baker's apprentice is granted three wishes by a mischievous genie but must use them wisely to outsmart an evil sorcerer.
- A young girl stumbles upon a hidden village inhabited by magical creatures and must help them save their enchanted home from a dark force.
- A magical key unlocks a hidden door, leading a young boy on an adventure

through a world of strange and fantastical beings.

- A queen with the gift of foresight struggles to protect her kingdom from a powerful sorceress who threatens to destroy all that she loves.
- A young prince with the ability to communicate with animals embarks on a quest to find his long-lost sister and restore harmony to their kingdom.
- A magical feather, carried by the wind, leads a heartbroken girl on a journey of self-discovery and healing.
- A wise old woman grants a young child a wish, but only if they can complete three seemingly impossible tasks.
- A kingdom cursed with endless night must rely on a brave adventurer to find the stolen sun and restore light to the land.

Short Story Writing Prompts

- A chance encounter at a coffee shop leads two strangers to discover an unexpected connection, altering the course of their lives.
- An elderly woman reminisces about her past as she watches her great-grandchild play, finding new meaning in her own life's journey.
- A futuristic society assigns everyone a job based on their aptitude; one individual refuses to conform, ultimately leading to a surprising revelation.
- A worn-out umbrella on a rainy day leads to an unexpected friendship between two lonely souls.
- An insomniac spends their sleepless nights exploring the city, uncovering its hidden beauty and ultimately finding peace within themselves.
- An inventor creates a device that allows them to communicate with animals, leading to humorous and

profound conversations about the nature of existence.

- A young boy, fascinated with the stars, forms a bond with a reclusive astronomer and learns that sometimes the most important discoveries are made within ourselves.
- A time traveler from the future accidentally arrives in the present day and must navigate our world while trying to find a way back home.
- A world-famous artist is struck with a sudden inability to create, leading them on a journey of self-discovery and unexpected inspiration.
- A lonely lighthouse keeper befriends a mysterious visitor who arrives during a violent storm, ultimately learning that not all storms are external.
- A struggling writer finds a diary hidden in the walls of their new

apartment, revealing the life and secrets of its former tenant and changing the writer's perspective forever.

- A magical bakery sells pastries that evoke specific memories, allowing customers to relive their happiest moments with each bite.
- Two siblings embark on a road trip to scatter their late father's ashes, rediscovering their bond and healing past wounds along the way.
- A mail carrier delivers a mysterious letter addressed to someone who no longer lives at the recipient's address, setting off a chain of events that connects multiple lives.
- A busker in a bustling city square plays an enchanting melody that touches the lives of those who stop to listen, transforming their day in unexpected ways.
- A chance discovery in a dusty old bookstore leads a woman on a

journey to unravel the secret history of her family.

- An overworked office employee discovers a hidden garden in the heart of the city, providing a much-needed escape and a newfound appreciation for life.
- An antique pocket watch passed down through generations is discovered to have the power to pause time, allowing its owner to explore the world around them in a new light.
- A persistent ringing phone in an empty apartment connects two strangers and leads to an unlikely friendship.
- A mysterious, old photograph found in a thrift store sparks a young woman's curiosity and sends her on a quest to uncover the story behind the image.
- A lonely man finds solace in feeding the birds at the local park,

discovering a connection to nature
that enriches his life.

- A weary traveler arrives at a quaint
  inn, only to find that the innkeeper
  has the uncanny ability to share the
  perfect story for each guest's needs.
- A mute street artist communicates
  with the world through their
  intricate and moving murals,
  touching the lives of those who
  encounter their work.
- A child with an uncanny ability to
  find lost things helps others
  reconnect with their own pasts and
  heal old wounds.
- A kind-hearted taxi driver provides
  an empathetic ear to their
  passengers, offering valuable
  insights and advice that leave a
  lasting impact on their lives.

Poetry Writing Prompts and Ideas

- A moment of transformation

- The ticking of time

- Nature's grandeur

- The human condition

- Love's passion

- The mourning process

- Childhood's wonder

- The power of dreams

- The complexity of identity

- The splendor of the night sky

- The art of letting go

- The journey to self-discovery

- The enchantment of the mundane

- The majesty of the sea

- The strength of hope

- The intricacy of relationships

- The beauty of the forest

- The resilience of the human spirit

- The awe of the sunrise

- The path of healing

- The potency of forgiveness

- The grandeur of the mountains

- The voyage of transformation

- The allure of the sunset

- The force of perseverance

- The beauty of the desert

- The journey of love

- The courage to overcome

- The elegance of a flower

- The quest for faith

- The power of acceptance

- The grace of a butterfly

- The journey through grief

- The strength of vulnerability

- The mystery of the universe

- The dance of the seasons

- The shadows of the past

- The search for belonging

- The ecstasy of laughter

- The essence of home

- The triumph of the human spirit

- The whisper of the wind

- The paradox of truth

- The depth of friendship

- The sparkle of a star

- The liberation of the mind

- The essence of a memory

- The harmony of music

- The power of the written word

- The magic of a first kiss

- The serenity of a garden

- The joy of parenthood

- The strength of a smile

- The beauty of a rainbow

- The path of self-acceptance

- The comfort of a warm embrace

- The power of determination

- The complexities of the human

  psyche

- The beauty of a snowflake

- The liberation of forgiveness

- The whispers of the heart

- The power of imagination

- The tenderness of love

- The rhythm of life

- The beauty of a hummingbird

- The struggle of mental illness

- The elegance of a swan

- The journey through fear

- The purity of innocence

- The majesty of an eagle

- The endurance of a marathon runner

- The secrets of the universe

- The beauty of a rainbow

- The essence of a dream

- The resilience of the human body

- The beauty of a daisy

- The ecstasy of discovery

- The beauty of a peacock

- The challenge of change

- The beauty of a waterfall

- The vulnerability of the human heart

- The power of the present moment

- The beauty of a summer breeze

- The complexities of the human condition

- The wisdom of experience

- The beauty of a butterfly's metamorphosis

- The dance of the tides

- The beauty of a sunrise over the mountains

- The courage of a soldier

- The beauty of a cherry blossom tree

- The journey through addiction

- The power of the human voice

- The beauty of a full moon

- The journey of self-improvement

- The beauty of a firefly's glow

- The mystery of the ocean depths

- The beauty of a shooting star

- The journey of growth

- The beauty of a city skyline

Random Creative Writing Prompts

- A protagonist who must confront their deepest fear
- A group of strangers stranded on a deserted island
- A romance between two people from rival families
- A young orphan who discovers a magical world
- A heist that goes wrong
- A mystery set in a small town
- A family drama centered around a long-lost relative
- A character who wakes up with no memory of the past year
- A protagonist who must overcome a physical disability to achieve their dreams
- A coming-of-age story set in a post-apocalyptic world
- A detective who must solve a murder case while dealing with personal issues

- A protagonist who travels back in time to fix a mistake
- A fantasy adventure set in a mythical world
- A tragedy of love and loss
- A character who must choose between love and duty
- A supernatural thriller centered around a haunted house
- A protagonist who must survive in a dystopian society
- A story set during a war
- A journey of self-discovery and personal growth
- A story of redemption and forgiveness
- A protagonist who must choose between loyalty and ambition
- A character who discovers a hidden talent
- A story about a forbidden love affair
- A science fiction story set on a distant planet

- A character who must confront their inner demons
- A protagonist who becomes a hero against all odds
- A protagonist who must escape from a dangerous situation
- A tale of revenge and justice
- A psychological thriller centered around a manipulative character
- A story about a family secret that is revealed
- A character who must make a difficult moral choice
- A character who must face their own mortality
- A historical fiction story set during a significant event in history
- A protagonist who must fight for their rights
- A character who discovers a hidden treasure
- A story about the power of friendship

- A protagonist who must escape from a false accusation
- A character who must confront a past trauma
- A romance between two people from different cultures
- A story about a journey of self-acceptance
- A story about a character who must learn to forgive themselves
- A protagonist who must overcome their own prejudices
- A story about a character who must navigate a toxic relationship
- A story about a character who must choose between their career and personal life
- A protagonist who must survive in a wilderness
- A story about a character who must choose between duty and passion
- A story about a character who must confront their own mortality

- A story about a character who must face a moral dilemma
- A story about a character who must make a difficult sacrifice
- A story about a character who must confront their own guilt
- A story about a character who must navigate a new culture
- A story about a character who must confront their own biases
- A story about a character who must navigate a difficult family dynamic
- A story about a character who must confront their own privilege
- A story about a character who must confront their own mental health issues
- A story about a character who must confront their own addiction
- A story about a character who must navigate a political landscape
- A story about a character who must navigate a complex legal system

- A story about a character who must navigate a religious landscape
- A story about a character who must navigate a new social environment
- A story about a character who must confront their own mortality
- A story about a character who must confront their own mortality
- A story about a character who must navigate a changing world
- A story about a character who must confront their own regrets
- A story about a character who must navigate a difficult work environment
- A story about a character who must navigate a failing marriage
- A story about a character who must navigate a complicated friendship
- A story about a character who must navigate a new identity
- A story about a character who must confront their own fears

- A story about a character who must navigate a legal battle
- A story about a character who must navigate a moral dilemma
- A story about a character who must navigate a cultural clash
- A story about a character who must navigate a difficult family reunion
- A story about a character who must navigate a difficult medical diagnosis
- A story about a character who must navigate a traumatic experience
- A story about a character who must navigate a difficult breakup
- A story about a character who must confront their own insecurities
- A story about a character who must navigate a complex business deal
- A story about a character who must navigate a toxic workplace
- A story about a character who must confront their own mortality
- A story about a character who must navigate a difficult pregnancy

- A story about a character who must navigate a difficult divorce
- A story about a character who must navigate a difficult adoption process
- A story about a character who must navigate a political scandal
- A story about a character who must navigate a cultural revolution
- A story about a character who must navigate a difficult custody battle
- A story about a character who must navigate a difficult immigration process
- A story about a character who must confront their own prejudices
- A story about a character who must navigate a difficult long-distance relationship
- A story about a character who must navigate a complex family inheritance
- A story about a character who must navigate a difficult addiction recovery process

- A story about a character who must navigate a difficult coming out process
- A story about a character who must confront their own mortality
- A story about a character who must navigate a difficult aging process
- A story about a character who must navigate a difficult professional transition
- A story about a character who must navigate a difficult natural disaster
- A story about a character who must navigate a difficult personal injury
- A story about a character who must navigate a difficult child custody battle
- A story about a character who must confront their own mortality
- A story about a character who must navigate a difficult diagnosis.
- A story about a character who must navigate a difficult decision about end-of-life care

- A story about a character who must confront their own trauma
- A story about a character who must navigate a difficult immigration process as a refugee
- A story about a character who must navigate a difficult legal battle against a corporation
- A story about a character who must navigate a difficult return to civilian life after serving in the military
- A story about a character who must navigate a difficult journey to find their birth parents
- A story about a character who must navigate a difficult journey to reunite with a lost love
- A story about a character who must confront their own toxic patterns in relationships
- A story about a character who must navigate a difficult transition from child to adult

- A story about a character who must navigate a difficult decision about whether to continue a pregnancy
- A story about a character who must navigate a difficult transition to retirement
- A story about a character who must navigate a difficult journey to overcome a phobia
- A story about a character who must navigate a difficult journey to become a parent
- A story about a character who must navigate a difficult journey to forgive a past hurt
- A story about a character who must navigate a difficult decision about whether to come out to their family
- A story about a character who must navigate a difficult decision about whether to keep a secret that could harm others

- A story about a character who must navigate a difficult decision about whether to testify in a court case
- A story about a character who must navigate a difficult journey to recover from a traumatic brain injury
- A story about a character who must navigate a difficult journey to heal from childhood abuse
- A story about a character who must navigate a difficult journey to overcome addiction to opioids
- A story about a character who must navigate a difficult journey to overcome addiction to alcohol
- A story about a character who must navigate a difficult journey to overcome addiction to gambling
- A story about a character who must navigate a difficult journey to overcome addiction to sex
- A story about a character who must navigate a difficult decision about

whether to go into witness protection

- A story about a character who must navigate a difficult journey to overcome a fear of public speaking
- A story about a character who must navigate a difficult journey to heal from a broken heart
- A story about a character who must navigate a difficult journey to heal from a physical injury
- A story about a character who must navigate a difficult journey to heal from a mental illness
- A story about a character who must navigate a difficult journey to find their place in the world
- A story about a character who must navigate a difficult journey to find their voice
- A story about a character who must navigate a difficult journey to find their purpose

- A story about a character who must navigate a difficult journey to find their faith
- A story about a character who must navigate a difficult journey to find their self-worth
- A story about a character who must navigate a difficult journey to find their creativity
- A story about a character who must navigate a difficult journey to find their courage
- A story about a character who must navigate a difficult journey to find their inner peace
- A story about a character who must navigate a difficult journey to find their true identity
- A story about a character who must navigate a difficult journey to find their true love
- A story about a character who must navigate a difficult journey to find closure

- A story about a character who must navigate a difficult journey to rebuild a broken relationship
- A story about a character who must navigate a difficult journey to reconnect with a lost friend
- A story about a character who must navigate a difficult journey to overcome a fear of flying
- A story about a character who must navigate a difficult journey to overcome a fear of water
- A story about a character who must navigate a difficult journey to overcome a fear of heights
- A story about a character who must navigate a difficult journey to overcome a fear of spiders
- A story about a character who must navigate a difficult journey to overcome a fear of the dark
- A story about a character who must navigate a difficult journey to overcome a fear of failure

- A story about a character who must navigate a difficult journey to overcome a fear of success
- A story about a character who must navigate a difficult journey to overcome a fear of commitment
- A story about a character who must navigate a difficult journey to overcome a fear of intimacy
- A story about a character who must navigate a difficult journey to overcome a fear of change
- A story about a character who must navigate a difficult journey to overcome a fear of rejection
- A story about a character who must navigate a difficult journey to overcome a fear of the unknown
- A story about a character who must navigate a difficult journey to overcome a fear of death
- A story about a character who must navigate a difficult journey to overcome a fear of public scrutiny

- A story about a character who must navigate a difficult journey to overcome a fear of being alone
- A story about a character who must navigate a difficult journey to overcome a fear of inadequacy
- A story about a character who must navigate a difficult journey to overcome a fear of abandonment
- A story about a character who must navigate a difficult journey to overcome a fear of success
- A story about a character who must navigate a difficult journey to overcome a fear of the future
- A story about a character who must navigate a difficult journey to overcome a fear of the past
- A story about a character who must navigate a difficult journey to overcome a fear of the present
- A story about a character who must navigate a difficult journey to overcome a fear of commitment

- A story about a character who must navigate a difficult journey to overcome a fear of change
- A story about a character who must navigate a difficult journey to overcome a fear of rejection
- A story about a character who must navigate a difficult journey to overcome a fear of failure
- A story about a character who must navigate a difficult journey to overcome a fear of success
- A story about a character who must navigate a difficult journey to overcome a fear of intimacy
- A story about a character who must navigate a difficult journey to overcome a fear of the unknown
- A story about a character who must navigate a difficult journey to overcome a fear of death
- A story about a character who must navigate a difficult journey to overcome a fear of public speaking

- A story about a character who must navigate a difficult journey to overcome a fear of spiders
- A story about a character who must navigate a difficult journey to overcome a fear of the dark
- A story about a character who must navigate a difficult journey to overcome a fear of heights
- A story about a character who must navigate a difficult journey to overcome a fear of water
- A story about a character who must navigate a difficult journey to overcome a fear of flying
- A story about a character who must navigate a difficult journey to overcome a fear of dogs
- A story about a character who must navigate a difficult journey to overcome a fear of thunderstorms
- A story about a character who must navigate a difficult journey to overcome a fear of driving

- A story about a character who must navigate a difficult journey to overcome a fear of social situations
- A story about a character who must navigate a difficult journey to overcome a fear of commitment
- A story about a character who must navigate a difficult journey to overcome a fear of love
- A story about a character who must navigate a difficult journey to overcome a fear of success
- A story about a character who must navigate a difficult journey to overcome a fear of failure
- A story about a character who must navigate a difficult journey to overcome a fear of rejection
- A story about a character who must navigate a difficult journey to overcome a fear of change
- A story about a character who must navigate a difficult journey to overcome a fear of public speaking

- A story about a character who must navigate a difficult journey to overcome a fear of heights
- A story about a character who must navigate a difficult journey to overcome a fear of spiders
- A story about a character who must navigate a difficult journey to overcome a fear of the dark
- A story about a character who must navigate a difficult journey to overcome a fear of water
- A story about a character who must navigate a difficult journey to overcome a fear of flying
- A story about a character who must navigate a difficult journey to overcome a fear of death
- A story about a character who must navigate a difficult journey to overcome a fear of intimacy
- A story about a character who must navigate a difficult journey to overcome a fear of the unknown

- A story about a character who must navigate a difficult journey to overcome a fear of abandonment
- A story about a character who must navigate a difficult journey to overcome a fear of inadequacy
- A story about a character who must navigate a difficult journey to overcome a fear of success
- A story about a character taking a road trip across the country
- A story about a character moving to a new city and starting over
- A story about a character traveling to a foreign country alone
- A story about a character who gets lost on a hike in a foreign country
- A story about a character who unexpectedly finds love while on vacation
- A story about a character who goes on a solo backpacking trip in the wilderness

- A story about a character who takes a trip to reconnect with their estranged family
- A story about a character who moves to a small town to escape their past
- A story about a character who takes a trip to find inspiration for their writing
- A story about a character who travels back in time to a different era
- A story about a character who takes a road trip with their best friend
- A story about a character who takes a trip to find their long lost sister
- A story about a character who travels to a foreign country to teach English
- A story about a character who takes a solo vacation to recharge their batteries
- A story about a character who moves to a new city to start a business
- A story about a character who takes a trip to the beach with their family

- A story about a character who moves to a new country for a job opportunity
- A story about a character who takes a trip to visit their dying grandfather
- A story about a character who goes on a spiritual retreat in the mountains
- A story about a character who takes a trip to meet their online lover for the first time
- A story about a character who moves to a new city to pursue their dream career
- A story about a character who takes a trip to reconnect with their ex
- A story about a character who travels to a foreign country to volunteer
- A story about a character who takes a trip to reconnect with their cultural roots

- A story about a character who moves to a new city to escape a toxic relationship
- A story about a character who takes a trip to the Grand Canyon with their friends
- A story about a character who travels to a foreign country to study abroad
- A story about a character who moves to a small town to start a family
- A story about a character who takes a trip to Europe to find their ancestors' homeland
- A story about a character who goes on a backpacking trip with their significant other
- A story about a character who takes a trip to heal after a breakup
- A story about a character who moves to a new city to start a new life after being released from prison

- A story about a character who travels to a foreign country to adopt a child
- A story about a character who takes a trip to Las Vegas with their best friends
- A story about a character who moves to a new city to escape their past and start fresh
- A story about a character who takes a trip to Bali to find inner peace
- A story about a character who travels to a foreign country to do research for a book
- A story about a character who moves to a small town to take care of their aging parent
- A story about a character who takes a trip to Jamaica to attend a friend's wedding
- A story about a character who goes on a backpacking trip with their siblings

- A story about a character who takes a trip to Paris to find love
- A story about a character who moves to a new city to start a new career
- A story about a character who takes a trip to Japan to explore their love for anime and manga
- A story about a character who travels to a foreign country to find their birth parents
- A story about a character who moves to a new city to attend college
- A story about a character who takes a trip to Iceland to see the Northern Lights
- A story about a character who goes on a camping trip with their extended family
- A story about a character who takes a trip to Hawaii to scatter their loved one's ashes
- A story about a character who travels to a foreign country to learn a new language

- A story about a character who moves to a new city to pursue their passion for music
- A story about a character who takes a trip to Mexico to reconnect with their heritage
- A story about a character who goes on a cruise with their significant other
- A story about a character who takes a trip to Alaska to work on a fishing boat
- A story about a character who travels to a foreign country to volunteer at an orphanage
- A story about a character who moves to a new city to start a new life with their partner
- A story about a character who takes a trip to Africa to volunteer at a wildlife sanctuary
- A story about a character who goes on a road trip with their estranged parent

- A story about a character who takes a trip to India to find inner peace and spirituality
- A story about a character who travels to a foreign country to find a cure for their rare disease
- A story about a character who moves to a new city to escape their abusive ex-partner
- A story about a character who takes a trip to New York to audition for a Broadway musical
- A story about a character who goes on a backpacking trip with their college friends
- A story about a character who takes a trip to Egypt to explore the pyramids and ancient history
- A story about a character who travels to a foreign country to compete in a sports tournament
- A story about a character who moves to a new city to pursue their dream of becoming an actor

- A story about a character who takes a trip to Australia to find adventure and excitement
- A story about a character who goes on a family vacation to a theme park
- A story about a character who takes a trip to Alaska to see the glaciers before they melt
- A story about a character who travels to a foreign country to reconnect with their estranged sibling
- A story about a character who moves to a new city to escape their mundane and unfulfilling life
- A story about a character who takes a trip to Thailand to explore their love for spicy food
- A story about a character who goes on a backpacking trip with their high school friends
- A story about a character who takes a trip to Greece to learn about their ancestors' history and culture

- A story about a character who travels to a foreign country to start a new business
- A story about a character who moves to a new city to join a new sports team
- A story about a character who takes a trip to the Amazon rainforest to experience the natural wonders
- A story about a character who goes on a romantic getaway with their partner
- A story about a character who takes a trip to Rome to explore the ancient architecture and art
- A story about a character who travels to a foreign country to start a new life as a digital nomad
- A story about a character who moves to a new city to join a startup company
- A story about a character who takes a trip to the Caribbean to experience the beach and island lifestyle

- A story about a character who goes on a hiking trip with their college professor
- A story about a character who takes a trip to Spain to learn flamenco dancing
- A story about a character who travels to a foreign country to adopt a pet
- A story about a character who moves to a new city to start a new life as an artist
- A story about a character who takes a trip to Antarctica to see the polar bears
- A story about a character who goes on a vacation to a luxurious resort with their significant other
- A story about a character who takes a trip to South Africa to experience the wildlife
- A story about a character who travels to a foreign country to find a new job

- A story about a character who moves to a new city to attend graduate school
- A story about a character who takes a trip to Ireland to explore their family's history
- A story about a character who goes on a camping trip with their childhood best friend
- A story about a character who takes a trip to Japan to learn about the tea ceremony
- A story about a character who travels to a foreign country to reunite with their long lost love
- A story about a character who moves to a new city to start a new life after a traumatic event
- A story about a character who takes a trip to Peru to see Machu Picchu
- A story about a character who goes on a skiing trip with their work colleagues

- A story about a character who takes a trip to Switzerland to experience the alps
- A story about a character who travels to a foreign country to attend a family member's wedding
- A story about a character who moves to a new city to pursue a career in fashion.

Character Creation

Writing Prompts and Ideas

- An artist who is struggling with creative block
- A politician who is torn between their personal values and their career ambitions
- A scientist who is on the brink of a groundbreaking discovery
- A social media influencer who is struggling to maintain their public image
- A detective who is haunted by a past case that they couldn't solve
- An athlete who is determined to win a major competition
- An adventurer who is seeking to explore the world's most dangerous terrain
- A chef who is determined to create a culinary masterpiece

- A teacher who is trying to make a positive difference in their students' lives
- An astronaut who is on a mission to explore the vast unknowns of space
- A journalist who is uncovering a major scandal
- A musician who is trying to make it big in the industry
- A soldier who is dealing with PTSD after serving in a war
- An environmentalist who is fighting to protect endangered species
- An inventor who is working on a revolutionary new technology
- A writer who is struggling to complete their first novel
- A scientist who is trying to find a cure for a deadly disease
- A photographer who is capturing the beauty of the world through their lens
- A lawyer who is fighting for justice in a high-profile case

- A firefighter who is putting their life on the line to save others
- A chef who is trying to run a successful restaurant despite the odds
- A soldier who is trying to adjust to civilian life after serving in the military
- A teacher who is dealing with difficult students in a challenging environment
- A musician who is trying to overcome stage fright
- A journalist who is struggling to remain objective in the face of bias and corruption
- An athlete who is dealing with a major injury that threatens their career
- An explorer who is braving the world's most extreme climates and environments
- A farmer who is struggling to make a living in a changing world

- An artist who is exploring new mediums and techniques to express themselves
- A scientist who is questioning the ethics of their research
- A wildlife conservationist who is fighting to protect natural habitats from destruction
- A writer who is dealing with writer's block
- A police officer who is navigating a complex case with personal connections
- A chef who is trying to win a major cooking competition
- An astronaut who is dealing with homesickness while in space
- A teacher who is trying to connect with a troubled student
- A musician who is dealing with the pressure of fame and success
- A journalist who is uncovering corruption within their own organization

- An athlete who is struggling with their mental health while competing at a high level
- A historian who is uncovering forgotten stories and events
- A social worker who is fighting to help those in need within a broken system
- A fashion designer who is trying to create a signature style that sets them apart
- A humanitarian aid worker who is working in a war-torn region
- A philosopher who is questioning the fundamental principles of their beliefs
- An environmental activist who is organizing protests and rallies to promote change
- A teacher who is trying to inspire a love of learning in their students
- A musician who is collaborating with other artists to create something new and innovative

- A writer who is dealing with criticism and rejection from publishers
- A lawyer who is fighting for the rights of marginalized communities
- A soldier who is trying to reconcile their experiences in
- An engineer who is developing a groundbreaking new technology
- A therapist who is helping clients overcome their traumas and mental health issues
- A marine biologist who is studying the impact of climate change on ocean life
- An archaeologist who is discovering lost artifacts and uncovering ancient civilizations
- A teacher who is helping students with learning disabilities succeed in the classroom
- An actor who is trying to break into the industry and land their big break

- A wildlife photographer who is capturing stunning images of endangered species
- A private investigator who is solving cases that the police can't crack
- An entrepreneur who is starting their own business and navigating the challenges of entrepreneurship
- A fashion model who is dealing with the pressures of the industry and the constant scrutiny of their appearance
- A detective who is working to solve a cold case that has gone unsolved for years
- A geologist who is studying the earth's natural formations and the history of the planet
- An artist who is struggling to balance their passion for art with the need to make a living
- A social worker who is advocating for the rights of foster children and finding them loving homes

- A pilot who is flying planes across the world and experiencing new cultures and landscapes
- A racecar driver who is competing in high-stakes competitions and pushing themselves to the limit
- A travel blogger who is exploring the world and sharing their adventures with others
- A surgeon who is performing life-saving operations and saving patients' lives
- A speech therapist who is helping clients overcome speech impediments and communicate effectively
- A film director who is bringing their vision to life on the big screen
- A video game designer who is creating immersive and innovative gaming experiences
- A biographer who is writing the story of a famous figure's life

- A disaster relief worker who is providing aid and support to communities affected by natural disasters
- A mountaineer who is climbing some of the world's tallest peaks and pushing themselves to their physical limits
- An astronaut who is dealing with isolation and loneliness while on a mission in space
- A volunteer who is dedicating their time and energy to a worthy cause
- An animal behaviorist who is studying the ways in which animals communicate and interact with each other
- A mediator who is helping to resolve conflicts and disputes between parties
- A racehorse trainer who is preparing their horses for high-stakes races and championships

- A motivational speaker who is inspiring others to achieve their dreams and overcome adversity
- A venture capitalist who is investing in promising new startups and entrepreneurs
- A meteorologist who is studying the weather patterns and predicting future weather events
- An urban planner who is designing cities and communities that are functional, sustainable, and livable
- A naturalist who is studying the ecology and wildlife of a specific region or ecosystem
- A historian who is researching and writing about a specific period or event in history
- A psychologist who is helping clients understand and overcome their personal challenges and mental health issues

- A professional gamer who is competing in tournaments and earning a living through gaming
- A pet groomer who is caring for and grooming pets of all kinds
- A sound engineer who is working to produce and record music for artists and bands
- A voice actor who is lending their voice to animate characters in movies, TV shows, and video games
- A wine sommelier who is educating others about the complexities and nuances of wine
- A park ranger who is protecting and preserving natural parks and wildlife habitats
- A wildlife rehabilitator who is caring for and rehabilitating injured
- A tour guide who is showing tourists the highlights of a city or region
- A stand-up comedian who is crafting jokes and performing for audiences

- A financial analyst who is helping clients manage their finances and investments
- A makeup artist who is creating stunning looks for clients in the entertainment industry
- A sports commentator who is providing analysis and commentary on games and matches
- A marine engineer who is designing and building ships and other marine structures
- A security consultant who is advising businesses and organizations on how to protect their assets and people.